It's a Match!

Sometimes things look alike. They are t

Draw a line to match the objects that are the **same**.

Sometimes things belong together even though they are **different**.

Draw a line to match the things that belong together.

SESAME STREET

Clean Up Time!

Some things are **different** sizes. Elmo has big toys and little toys. He wants to sort all his toys by size and put them away.

Draw a line from each big toy to the big box.
Draw a line from each small toy to the small box.

Explore More

Sorting is a good way to help your child learn about how things are **different** and how they are the **same.** Fill a big box or laundry basket with items and encourage your child to sort the items in **different** ways: by color; by size; by shape; by which family member it belongs to; or by category (for example: toys with toys, books with books, clothes with clothes). Your child can draw pictures of big things, red things, or square things too.

It's All the Same to Me!

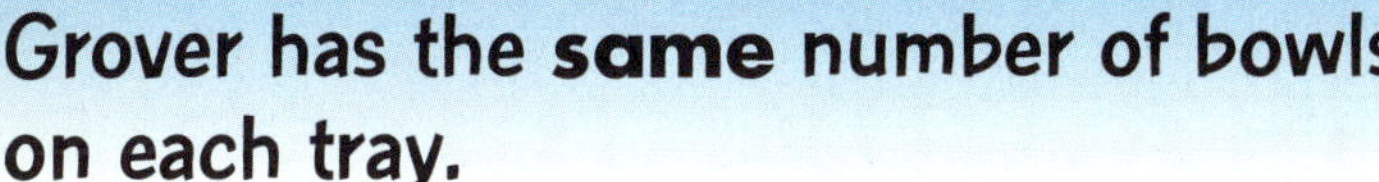

Grover has the **same** number of bowls on each tray.

Count the objects in each group. Then circle the two groups in each row that have the **same** number of objects.

Small, Smaller, Smallest

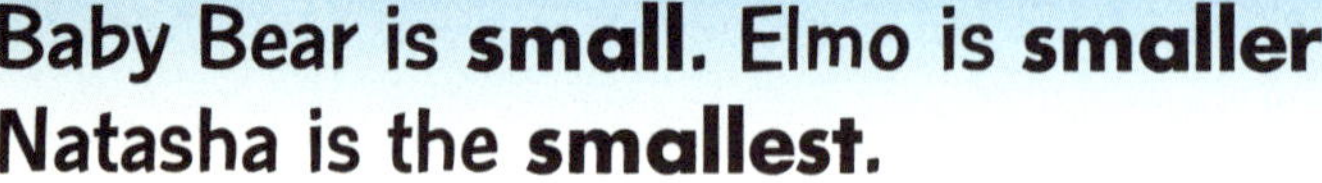

Baby Bear is **small**. Elmo is **smaller**.
Natasha is the **smallest**.

Circle the object in each row that is the **smallest**.

Draw and color a picture of something that is **smaller** than you.

Big, Bigger, Biggest

These friends are different sizes! Ernie is **big**. Cookie Monster is **bigger**. Big Bird is the **biggest** of all.

Color the object in each row that is the **biggest**.

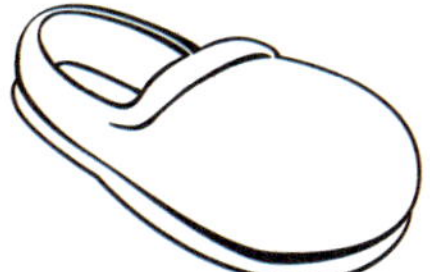

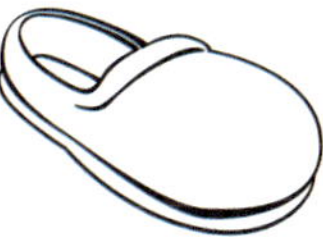

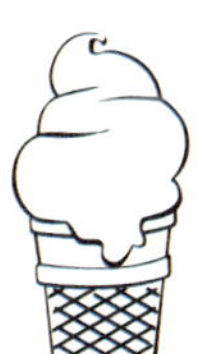

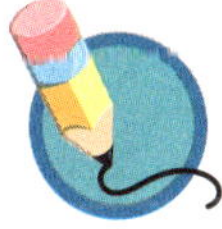

Draw and color a picture of something that is **bigger** than you.

Which has Less?

Ernie's blue bottle of bubble bath has **less** bubble bath in it than the other green bottle.

Look at the objects in each group. Then color the group in each row with **less**.

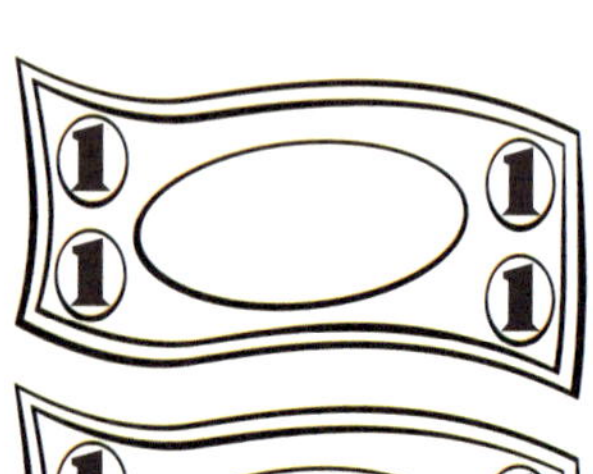

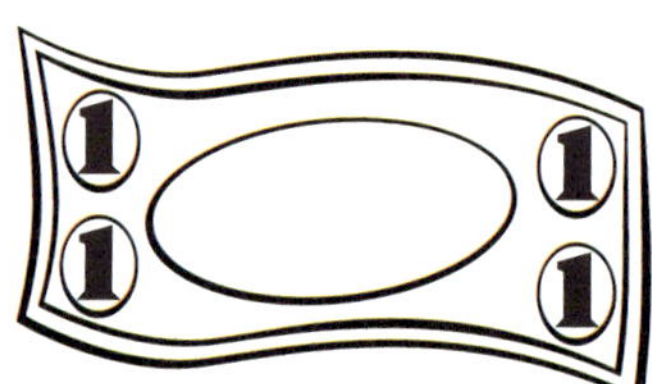

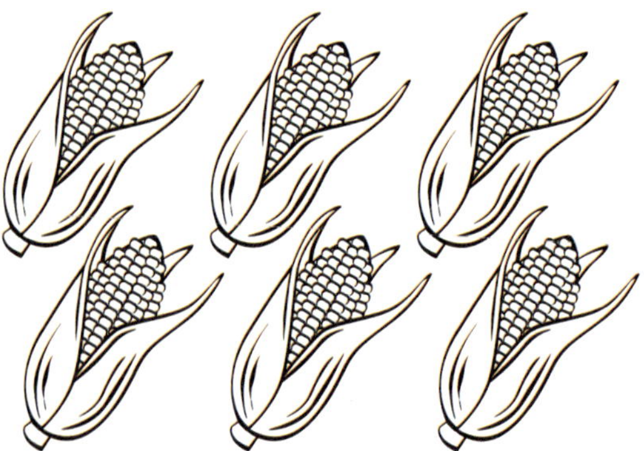

Which Has More?

Abby Cadabby is sitting on the pile with **more** pumpkins.

Count the objects in each group. Then circle the group in each row with **more**.

Explore More

Use snack time as an opportunity to reinforce the concepts of **more**, and the **same**. For example, put some crackers on two plates, and ask your child which one has **more**. Put some apple slices on one plate for her and on another for you; ask her to help you place the **same** number of apples on each plate.

The Same Game

Zoe has 2 balls. Elmo has 2 flippers. They both have 2! They have the same number of things!

Count the objects in each group. Then draw a line to match the groups that have the **same** number of objects.

Home, Sweet Home

Draw a line to connect the dots from **1–20** to see where the Count is standing.

Color the picture.

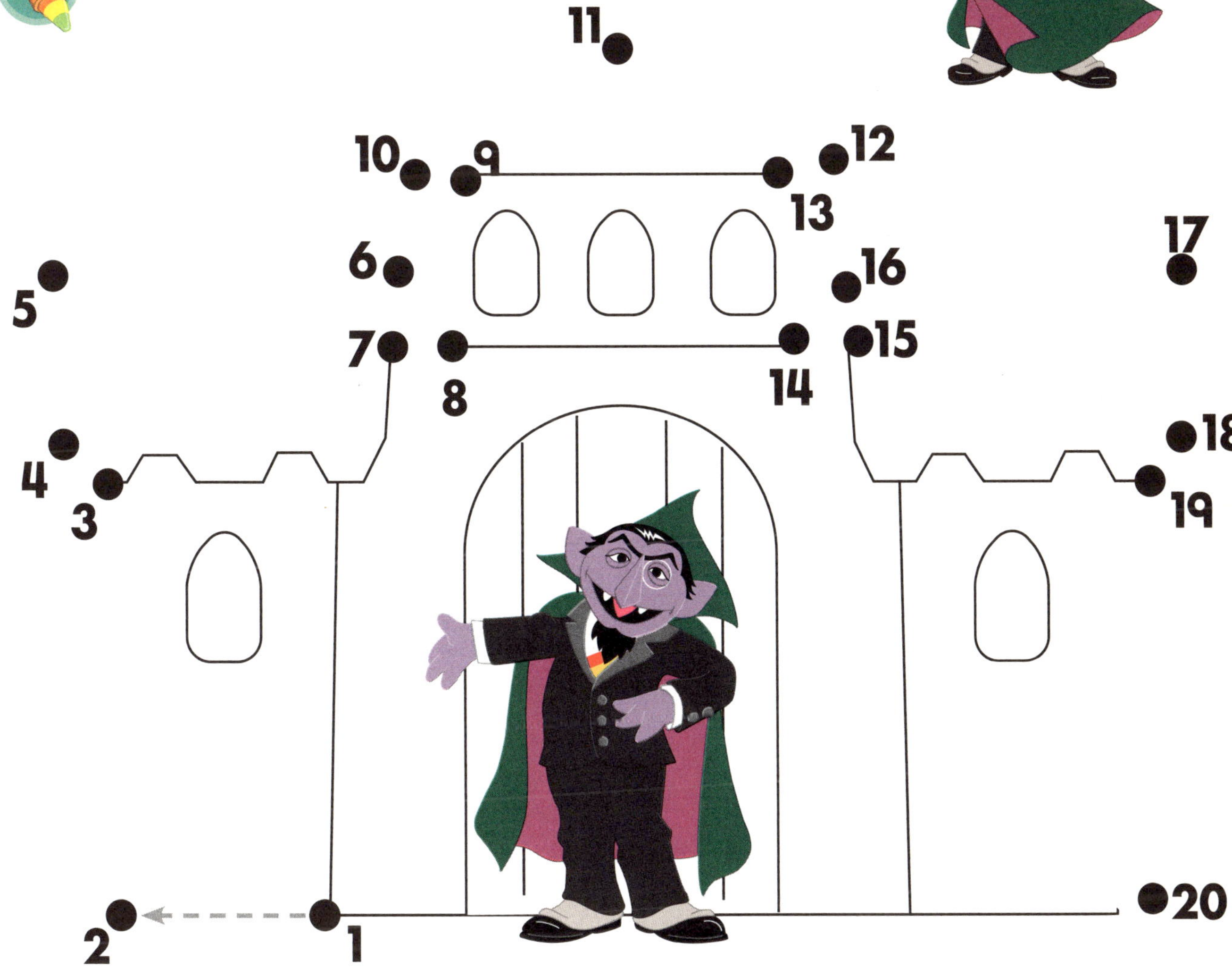

11

10 9 12

13

6 16 17

5

7 8 15

14

4 18

3 19

2 1 20

Explore More

Make a set of number cards with your child, mix them up, and encourage him to put the cards in order from 1-10. See if he can put them in order backwards from 10-1. Make it a countdown race to see how fast he can do it. When he is ready, add the numbers 11-20 to the card set.

Get to Know The Numbers

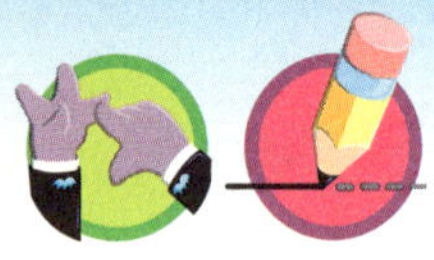

Count the things in each group. Then trace each number to show how many.

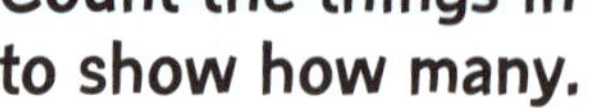

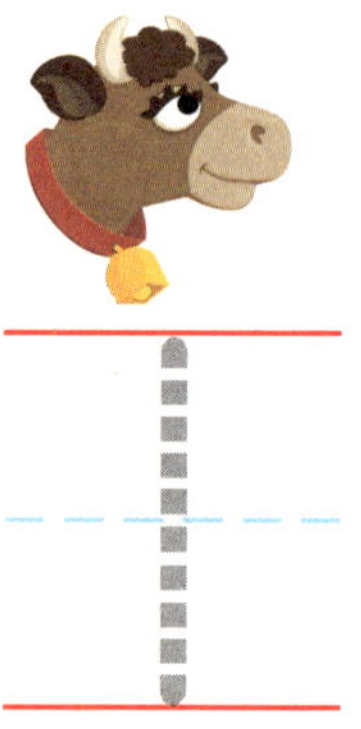

1

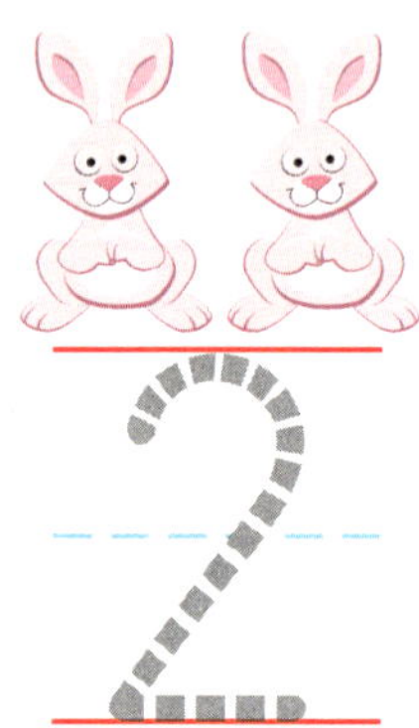

2

3

4

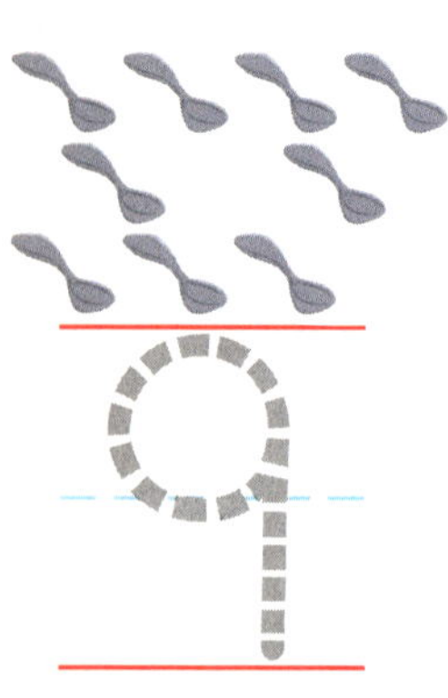

9

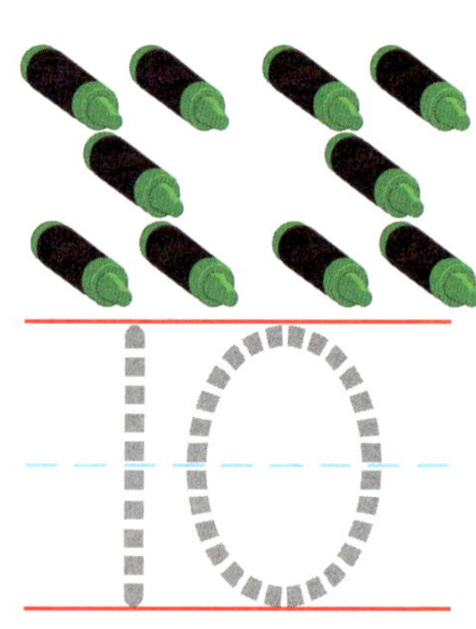

10

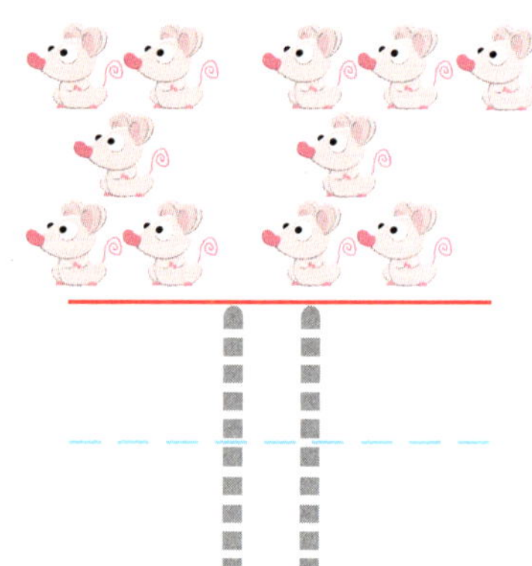

11

12

16

17

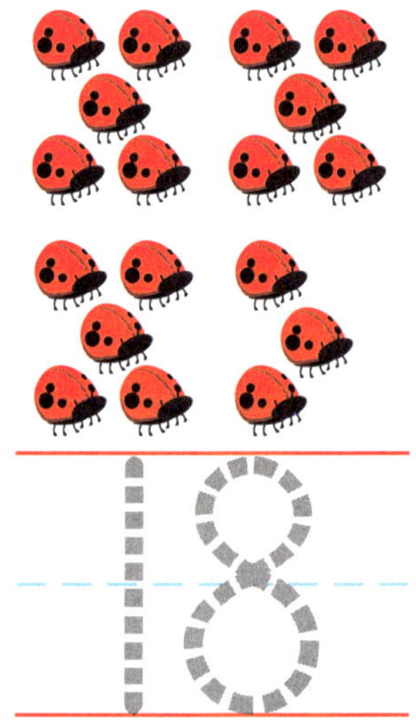

18

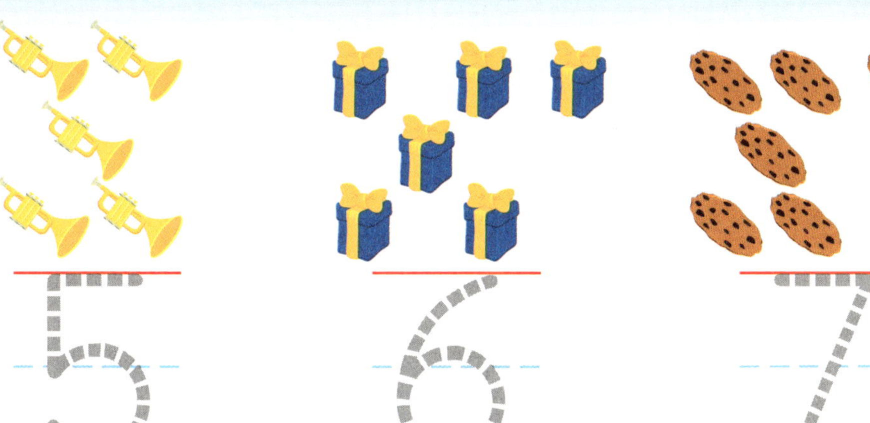
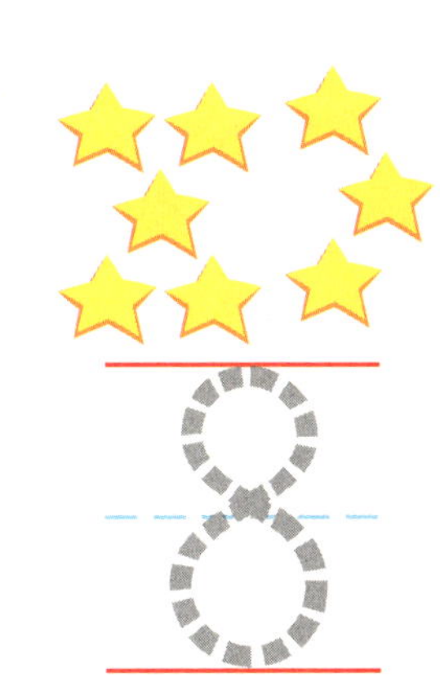

5 6 7 8

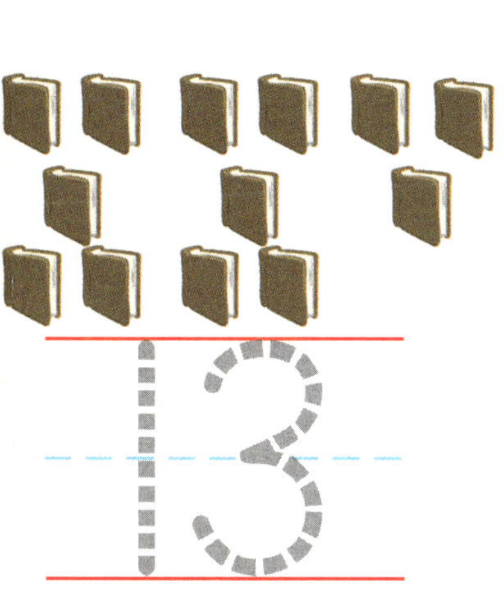

13 14 15

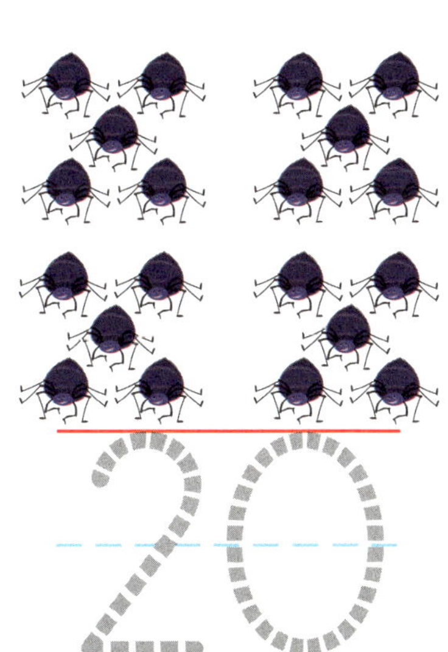

19 20

Count to 20

Ernie likes to count with Rubber Duckie.
Squeak, squeak!

Say the numbers from **1–20**.
Write in the missing numbers.

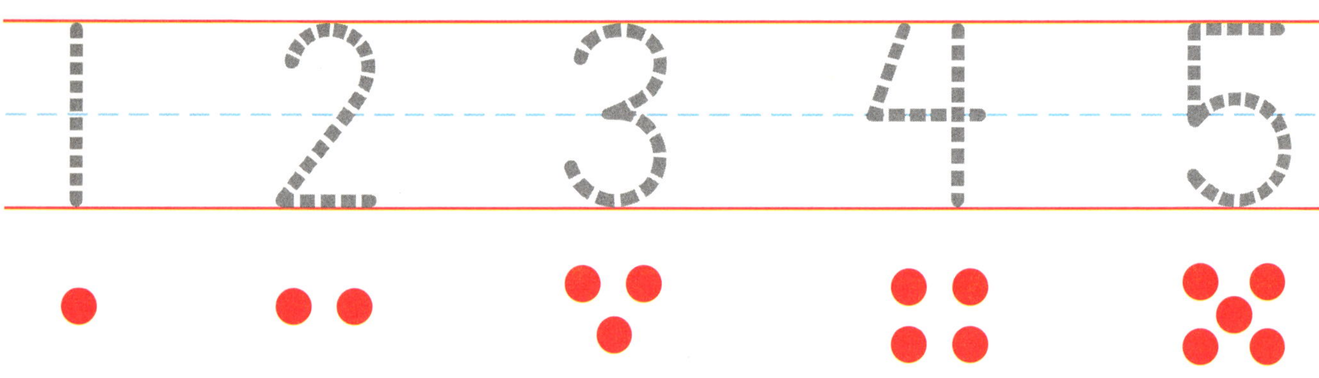

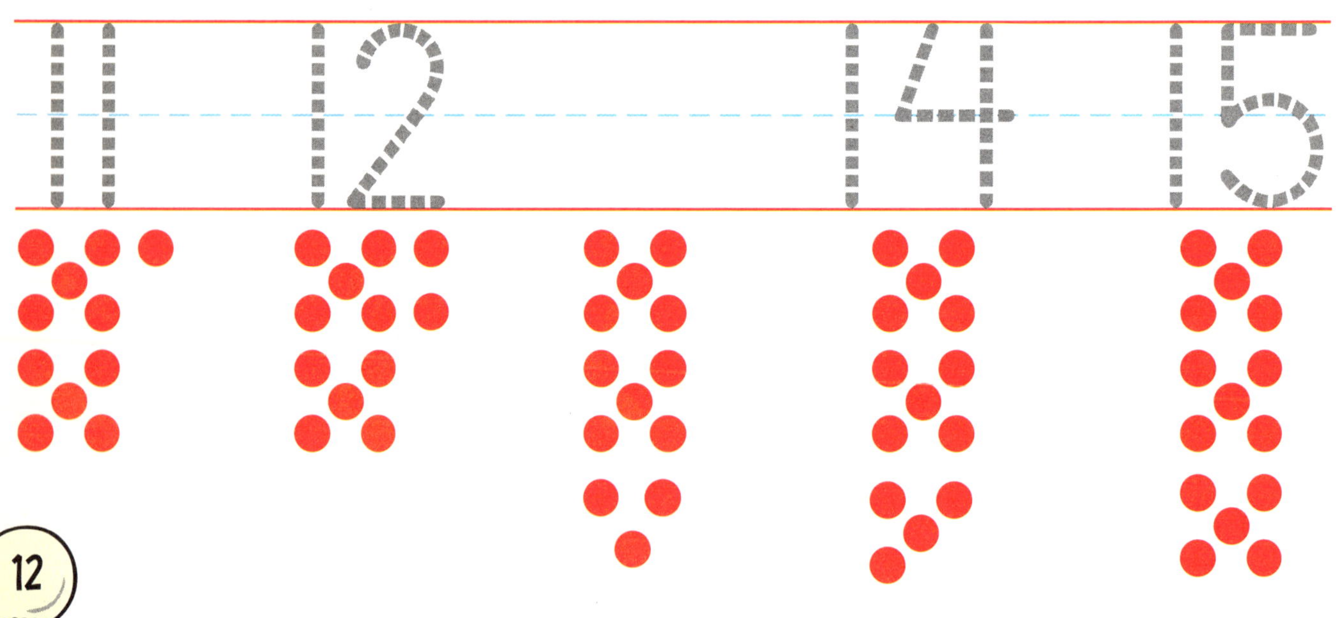

Bert and Bernice keep counting, all the way to **20**.

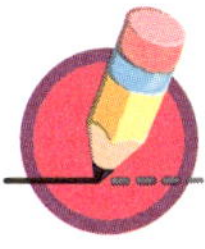

Count the dots under each number.
Then, trace the number.

6 7 9 10

16 18 19 20

Ready, Set, Lift-off!

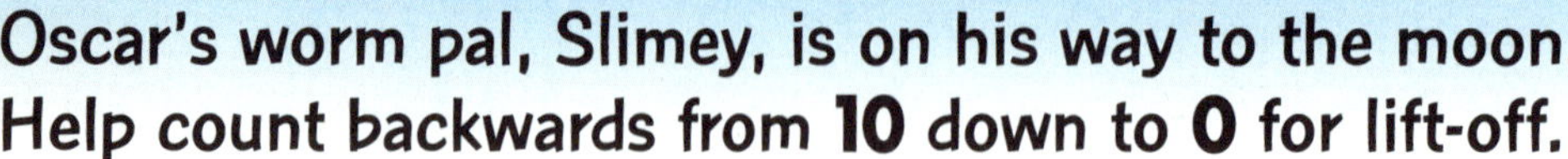

Oscar's worm pal, Slimey, is on his way to the moon. Help count backwards from **10** down to **0** for lift-off.

Draw a line to connect the dots from **10** down to **0**.

Say the numbers as you count backwards. Then color the picture.

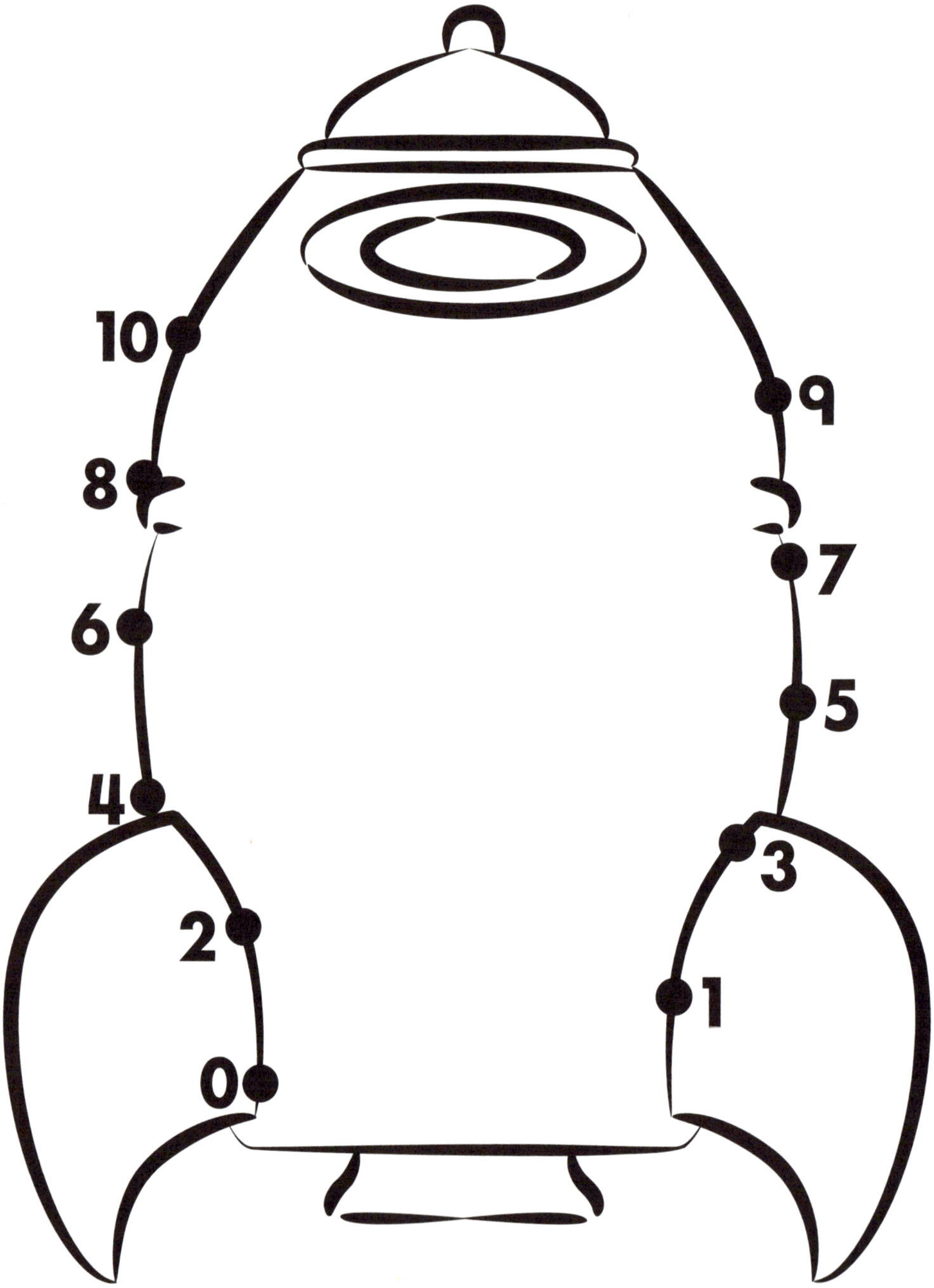

Happy Birthday, Elmo!

Elmo got a present for his birthday!

Draw a line to connect the dots backwards from **20-0** to see Elmo's gift.

Say the numbers as you count backwards. Then color the picture.

Explore More

Practice counting backwards! Try showing your child how to count backwards until the cookies are done baking, or until someone arrives home, or as she races to get dressed in the morning. Or, draw a number line on the sidewalk with chalk, and have your child jump backwards as she says the numbers from **20-0**.

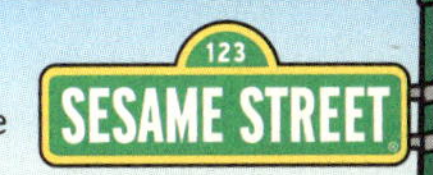

Who's First? Who's Last?

Zoe is **first** in line. Rosita is **next**. Elmo is **last**.

Circle the friend who is **first** in each row.
Color the friend who is **last** in each row.

Ride With Us!

Grover is **1st**. Rosita is **2nd**. Ernie is **3rd**.

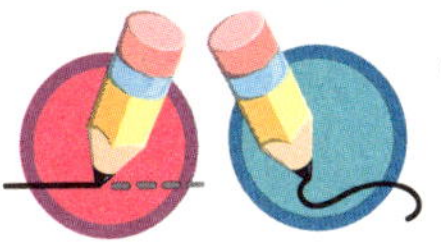

Trace over the numbers on each car of the roller coaster. Then draw yourself in the **3rd** car!

Use the color key below to color the cars.

1st **2nd** **3rd**

Explore More

Have your child practice **1st**, **2nd**, and **3rd** with stuffed animals or other friends. Encourage him to line up 3 stuffed animals in a row. Then you may ask a question like, "Who is **1st**?" Or, give your child clues and encourage him to put the animals in the order that you suggest. For example, you might say, "Please place the green animal **1st**, the yellow animal **2nd**, and the brown animal **3rd**."

Shape Up!

Rosita is learning all about shapes.

Trace each shape. Then draw some of your own.

circle

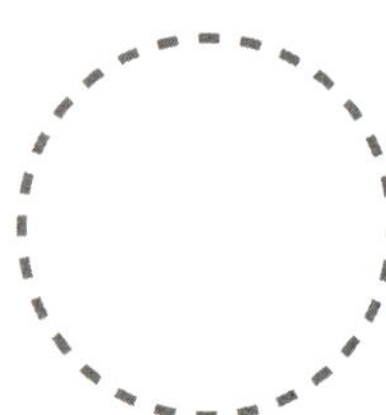

oval

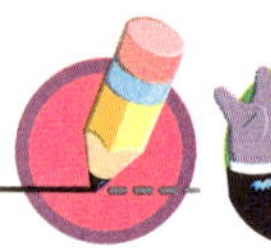

Trace each shape. Count the sides on each shape as you trace.

rectangle

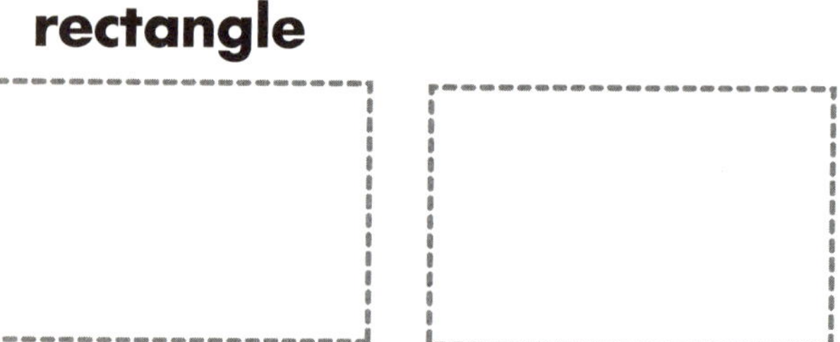

rhombus

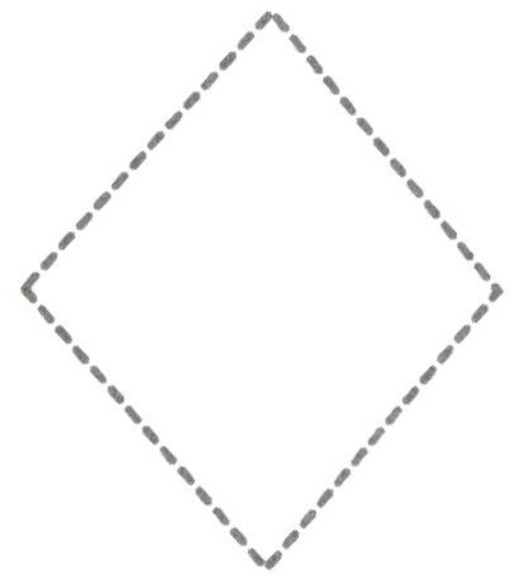

square

pentagon

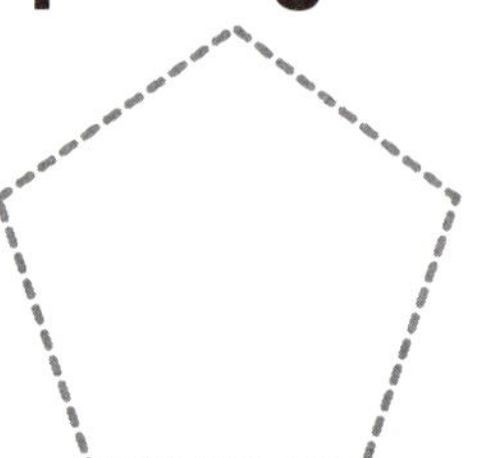

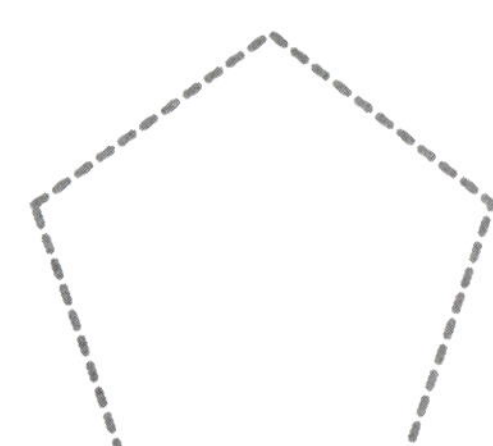

triangle

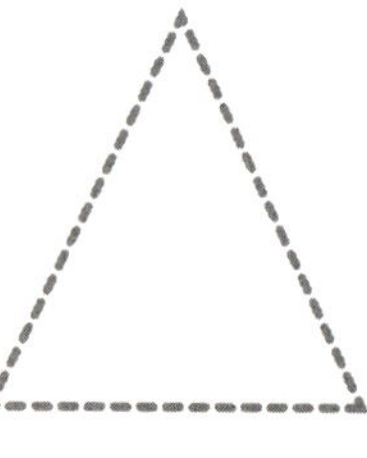

hexagon

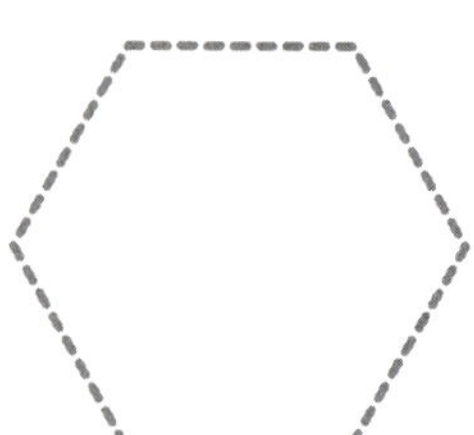

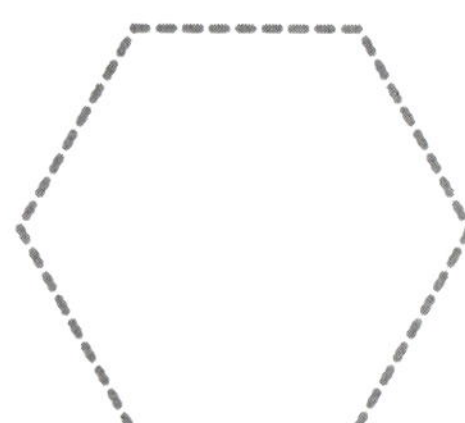

A Friend for Dorothy

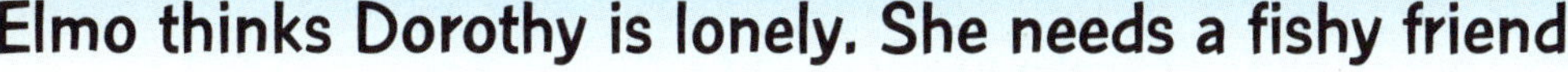

Elmo thinks Dorothy is lonely. She needs a fishy friend.

  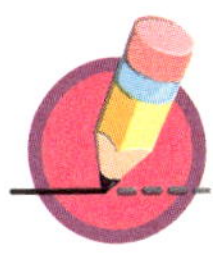 Count the fish in each bowl and trace each number below.

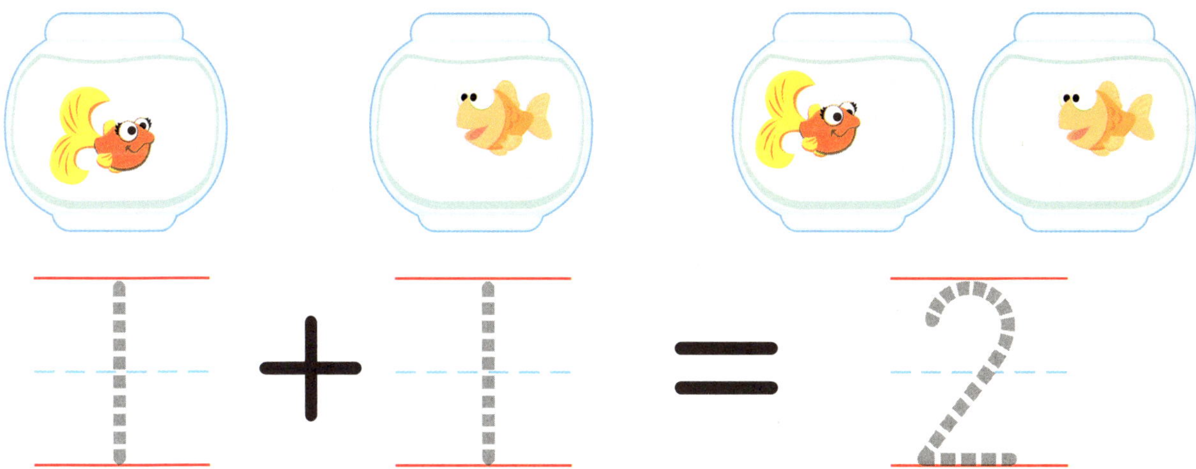

1 Dorothy plus **1** more fish friend-that's **2** fish all together!

Now Elmo needs to feed his fishy friends 1 food flake for each friend.

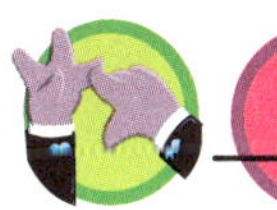 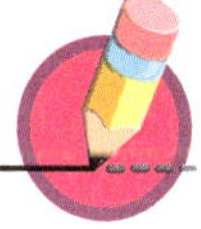 Count the flakes in each group and trace each number below.

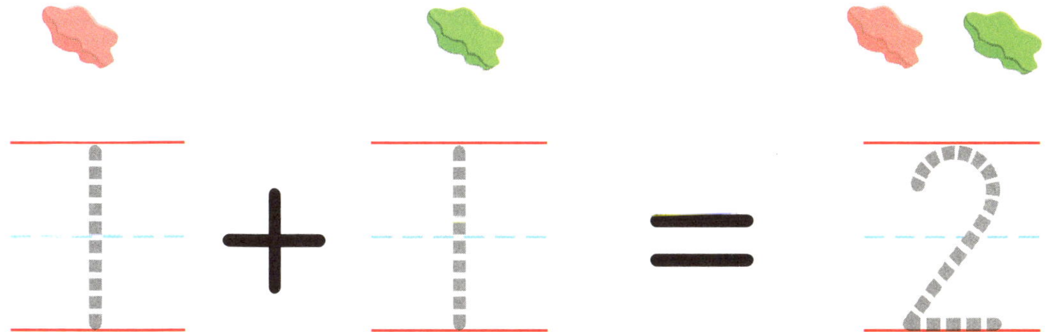

1 food flake for Dorothy plus **1** food flake for her friend - that's **2** food flakes all together!

Add It Up

Count the objects in each group. Draw a picture at the end that shows how many all together.

2 1

1 4

3 2

1 3

Friends for Bernice

Bert likes to bird-watch with his friend, Bernice. Here come some of Bernice's friends!

  Count the birds in each group and write each number below.

1 Bernice + **2** friends = **3** pigeons all together.

   Count Bernice and all her friends. Write the number to show how many birds there are all together.

 +     =

1 **4**

1 Bernice and **4** bird friends - that's **5** pigeons all together. You are adding!

Beach Fun

There are so many ways to play at the beach!

Color the first group of objects. Color **1** more.
Count and write how many **all together**.

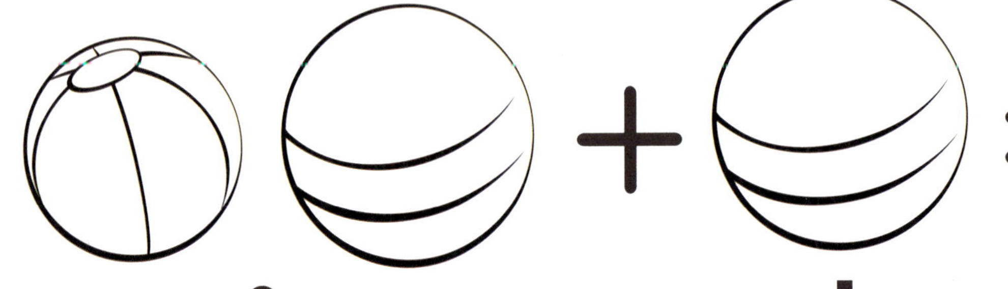

2 + 1 = ____

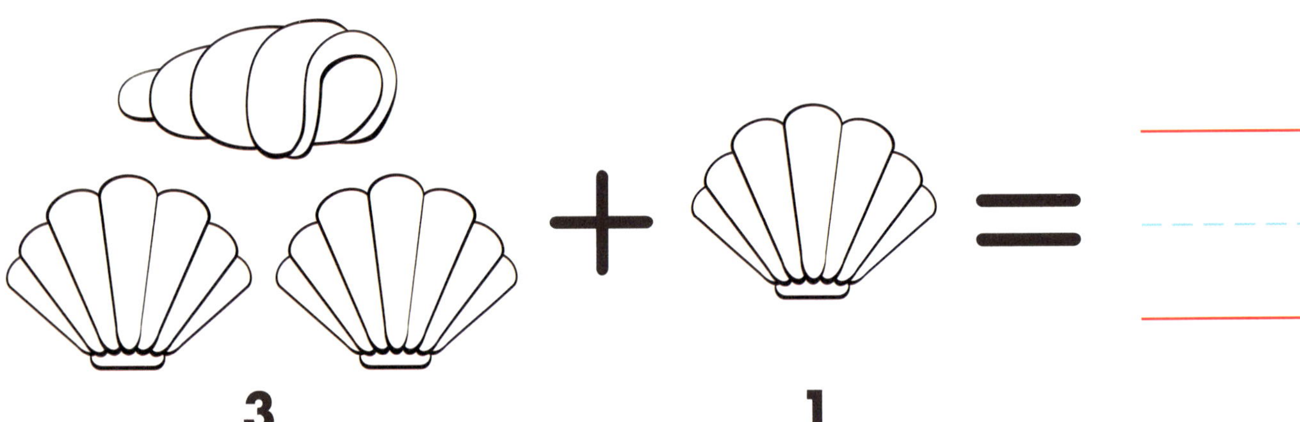

3 + 1 = ____

4 + 1 = ____

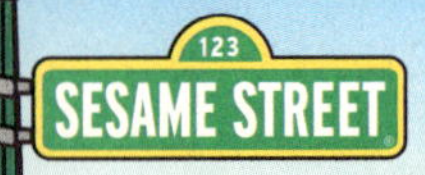

Fly Away, Fairies!

Abby Cadabby is having fun with some friendly fairies. But wait, some are flying away!

Count the fairies. Then draw an **X** on **2** that are flying away. Write how many are left.

4 — 2 = ____

3 — 2 = ____

5 — 2 = ____

Me Want COOKIE!

Cookie Monster sees a plate with **2** cookies.
He wants to eat **1** cookie.

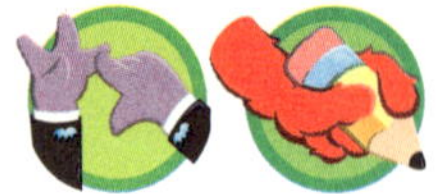

Count the cookies on each plate and write each number below. Then write how many are left.

 — 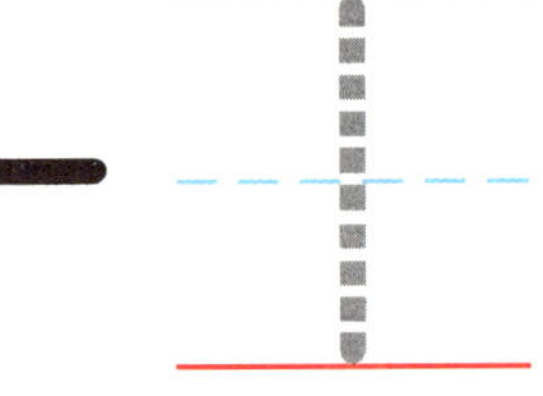 = 

2 cookies take away **1** cookie leaves **1** cookie.

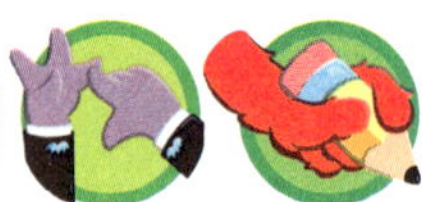

Count the cookies on each plate and write each number below. Then write how many are left.

— =

4 cookies take away **2** cookies leaves **2** cookies.

Explore More

Practice subtraction like Cookie Monster! Place a few food items (like crackers, carrot sticks, or slices of cheese) on a plate. Have your child count how many are on the plate. Then, take some of the items away and have him count them again. Repeat the numbers as you practice and count. For example, you might say, "There were **4** crackers. I took away **2**, how many are left?"

Your Soup, Sir!

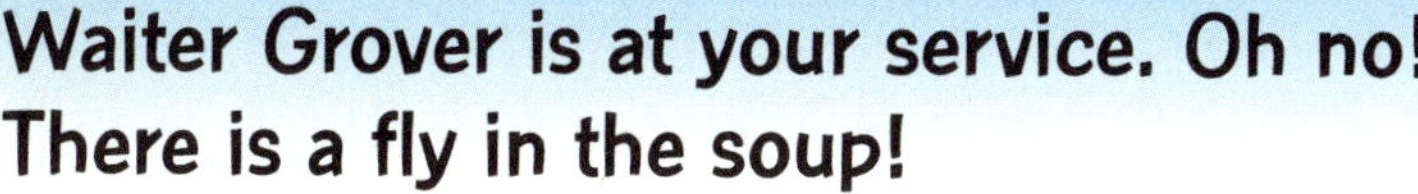

Waiter Grover is at your service. Oh no!
There is a fly in the soup!

Count all the bowls of soup. Draw an **X** on each bowl that has a fly in it. Count how many bowls are left and write the number.

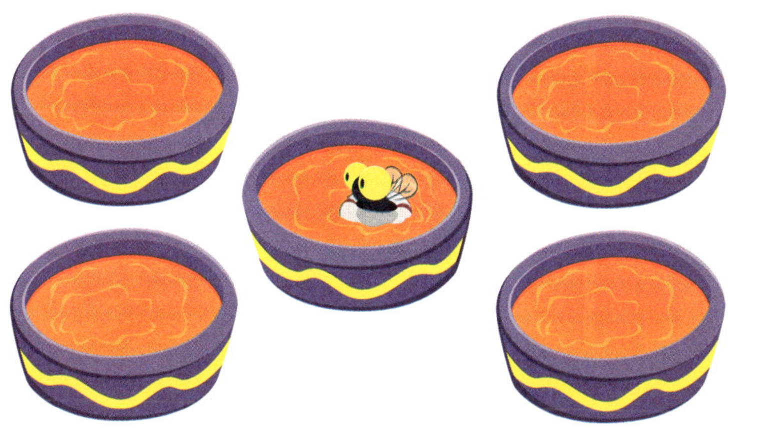

5 − 1 = ____

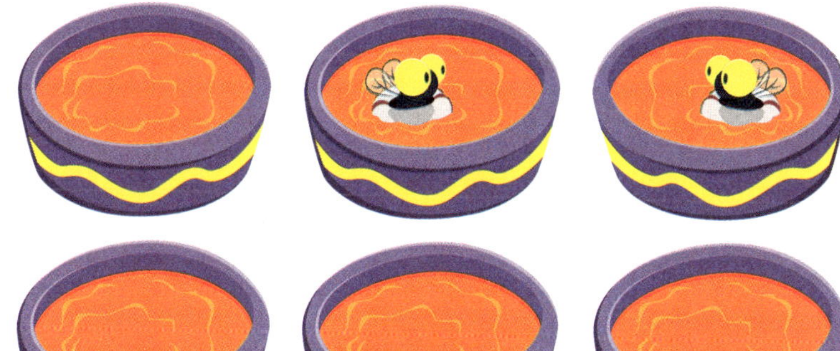

6 − 2 = ____

Where Did All the Fish Go?

Ernie is swimming with some fish.
The **blue** fish keep swimming away.

Count all the fish. Draw an **X** on the **blue** fish. Count how many fish are left and write the number.

5 – 2 = ______

6 – 3 = ______

4 – 1 = ______

6 – 2 = ______

The Gang's All Here!

Ernie and Bert are playing outside. Zoe and Elmo want to play, too.

Count the friends in each group and write each number below the picture. Write how many friends there are **all together**.

____ + ____ = ____

Bert has to go home to feed Bernice.

Count the friends. Circle the friend who is going home. Write how many friends will stay and play.

____

Hooray for You!

Elmo is playing adding tic tac toe.

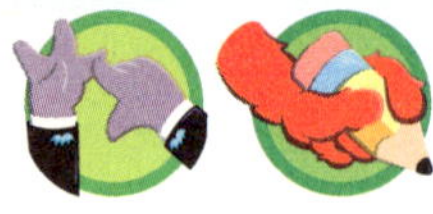

Count the things in each group and write how many **all together**. Draw a line through three numbers that are the same.

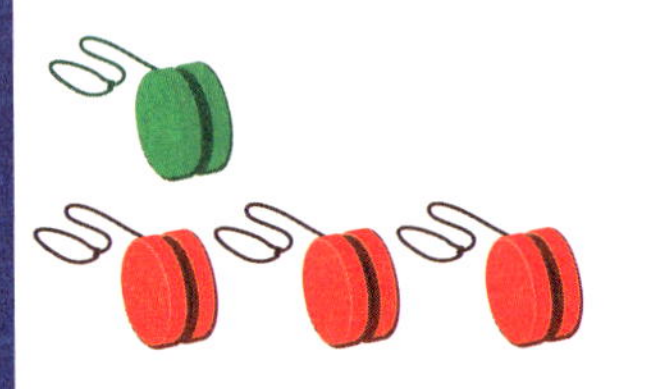

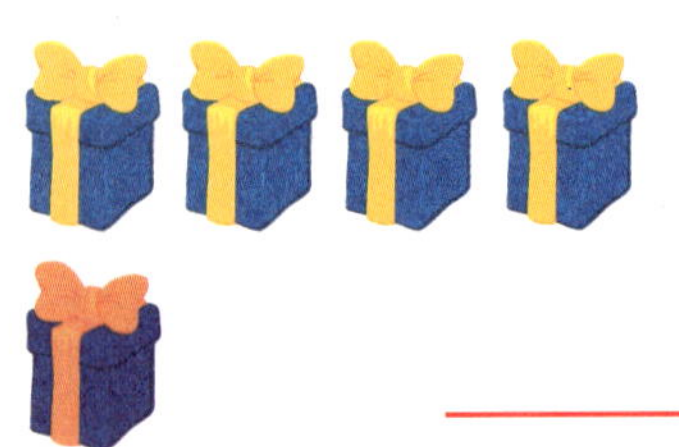

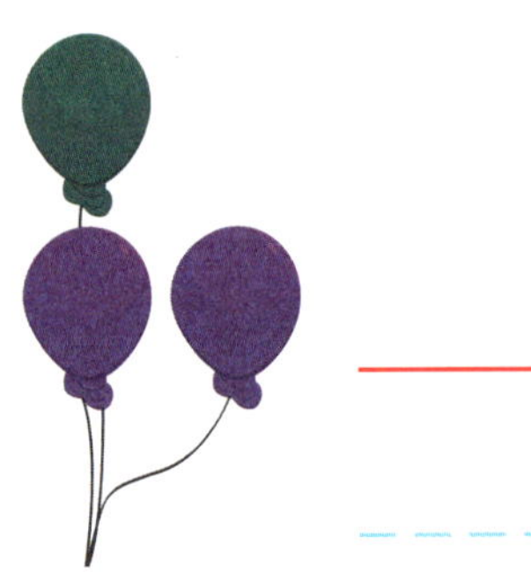

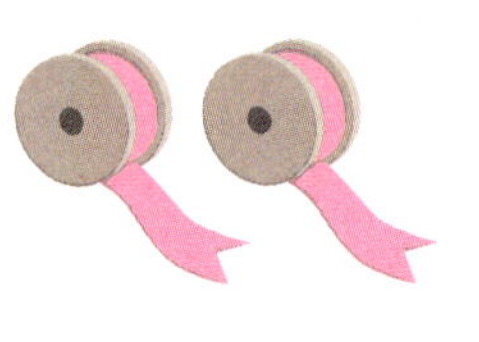

Great adding! You are a math champ! What else can you add?